~ FIRST GREEK MYTHS ~
PEGASUS THE FLYING HORSE

For Peter B
S.P.
To all my boys
J.L.

LONDON BOROUGH TOWER HAMLETS	
C001589880	
HJ	07/08/2008
TALES	£4.99
CANID	

ORCHARD BOOKS
338 Euston Road, London NW1 3BH
Orchard Books Australia
Level 17/207 Kent Street, Sydney NSW 2000
This text was first published in the form of a gift collection
called *First Greek Myths* by Orchard Books in 2003
This edition first published in hardback by Orchard Books in 2008
First paperback publication in 2009
Text © Saviour Pirotta 2008
Cover illustrations © Jan Lewis 2008
Inside Illustrations © Jan Lewis 2008
The rights of Saviour Pirotta to be identified as the author and
of Jan Lewis to be identified as the illustrator of this work
have been asserted by them in accordance with the
Copyright, Designs and Patents Act, 1988.
A CIP catalogue record for this book is available from the British Library.
ISBN 978 1 84616 473 6 (hardback)
ISBN 978 1 84616 771 3 (paperback)
1 3 5 7 9 10 8 6 4 2 (hardback)
1 3 5 7 9 10 8 6 4 2 (paperback)
Orchard Books is a division of Hachette Children's Books,
an Hachette Livre UK company.
Printed in China

www.orchardbooks.co.uk

~ FIRST GREEK MYTHS ~
PEGASUS THE FLYING HORSE

BY SAVIOUR PIROTTA
ILLUSTRATED BY JAN LEWIS

ORCHARD BOOKS

~ CAST LIST ~

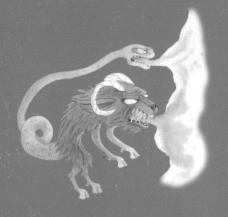

THE CHIMERA
(Kai-mee-rah)

BELLEROPHON
(Bell-er-o-phon)

What a hideous monster the chimera was! It had the head of a lion, the body of a goat and the tail of a snake.

When it opened its mouth, long flames reached out and burned anything in their way. Everyone in the land was scared of it.

"I must stop this creature frightening my people," said the king. "Bring me Bellerophon!"

Bellerophon was the bravest man in the country, but even he started trembling when he heard the king's request. Bellerophon knew that the only way to kill the chimera was with magic. So he went to see a wise magician.

"The chimera is indeed a very dangerous creature," said the wise magician. "No one who has ever tried to kill it has lived to tell the tale."

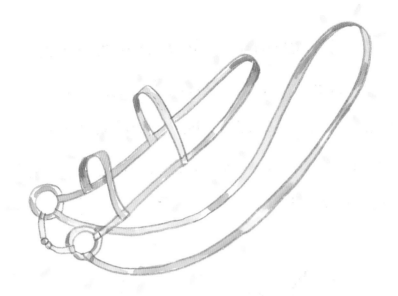

The magician took a golden
bridle from a cupboard. "The only
way to approach the monster is
from above," he said. "Take this
to the hills and find the flying
horse Pegasus. He is wild and
dangerous, but if you throw this
magic bridle over him, you will be
able to ride on his back."

"Then I could fly over the chimera and kill it with my spear," said Bellerophon.

He put the bridle over his shoulder and strode off.

On the way, he stopped at a village to ask where he could find Pegasus. But no one had heard of the flying horse.

Then a small boy stepped forward and said, "Every night when the moon is shining brightly, Pegasus lands to drink from a spring in the hills."

"We've seen him," added his
sister. "He stays on the ground for
a few seconds, then he's back up
in the air."

Bellerophon found the spring that the children had told him about and hid behind a bush. He waited but there was no sign of Pegasus.

Soon Bellerophon began to feel
tired until eventually he fell
fast asleep.

In the morning he was woken
by the shouts of the children.

"Look! Pegasus has been here!"
they cried and pointed at
hoofprints in the mud.

That night, Bellerophon went without supper so that his hunger would keep him awake.

Just after midnight, he heard
the flapping of wings and the
clip-clopping of hooves. Pegasus!

Slowly, Bellerophon crept forward. When he was standing right behind the horse, he threw the magic bridle around his neck.

Pegasus reared up and pawed
the ground, but it was no use – he
was caught. Bellerophon jumped
on his back.

It didn't take long to find the chimera's lair, but the monster had heard them coming. It rushed out of its cave howling, with bright, hot flames shooting out of its mouth.

Bellerophon had never seen
such a horrid creature. He would
never be able to kill it with his
spear alone. There had to be
another way.

Just then, Bellerophon saw
a lead mine close to the chimera's
lair. He pulled on Pegasus's reins
and the horse dived gracefully to
the ground.

Quickly, Bellerophon picked up
a heavy lump of lead. He pulled
on the reins again and Pegasus
soared back up into the sky.

Bellerophon looked down at the chimera in front of its dark cave. He stuck the lump of lead on the tip of his spear and shouted at the top of his voice. "Now!"

Pegasus dived at full speed towards the chimera, ducking to avoid the burning flames.

Bellerophon hurled his spear
right into the monster's fiery
mouth. Suddenly, the chimera's
eyes bulged. The lead had melted
in its throat and was poisoning it.

28

The monster fell to the ground.
It was dead at last.

Bellerophon and Pegasus flew
off in triumph.

Now everyone in the country
could live in peace and without
fear for the rest of their lives.

~ FIRST GREEK MYTHS ~

PEGASUS THE FLYING HORSE

BY SAVIOUR PIROTTA ~ ILLUSTRATED BY JAN LEWIS

And enjoy a little magic with these First Fairy Tales:

First Greek Myths and First Fairy Tales are available from all
good bookshops,or can be ordered direct from the publisher:
Orchard Books, PO BOX 29, Douglas IM99 1BQ
Credit card orders please telephone 01624 836000
or fax 01624 837033
or e-mail: bookshop@enterprise.net for details.

To order please quote title, author and ISBN
and your full name and address.
Cheques and postal orders should be
made payable to 'Bookpost plc'.
Postage and packing is FREE within the UK
(overseas customers should add £1.00 per book).

Prices and availability are subject to change.